THE SEED
OF COMPASSION

Lessons from the Life and Teachings of His Holiness the Dalai Lama

by His Holiness the Dalai Lama

illustrations by **Bao Luu**

Kokila

Kokila

An imprint of Penguin Random House LLC, New York

Visit us online at penguinrandomhouse.com

Library of Congress Control Number: 2019954593

Printed in the United States of America
ISBN 9780525555148

1 3 5 7 9 10 8 6 4 2

Design by Jasmin Rubero
Text set in Bembo Infant MT

The art for this book was created digitally.

THE DALAI LAMA

I have had the opportunity to travel to many countries, during which I have met and spoken to many children. As I won't have the opportunity to personally meet all the children of the world, it brings me great joy to share this story with you, my young brothers and sisters.

In this book, I recount memories of my childhood and share lessons I learned from my mother and others who have helped me cultivate the seed of compassion that we all possess. I hope this story will help that seed flourish within each of you and contribute to a more compassionate world with a sense of oneness of humanity.

November 25, 2019

I was born in Taktser, in the Amdo province of northeastern Tibet. It was a place of tall mountains, clear streams, blue skies, and many animals—mastiffs, sheep, horses, yaks, scorpions, chickens, and cows.

Our home was in the shadow of the Ami-chiri, The Mountain That Pierces the Sky.

Mine was a family of farmers. My father would spend the day tending to and selling horses, and I would stay home with my mother and help with her daily work.

We would plant barley, buckwheat, and potatoes. But those were not the only seeds we planted. From the time I was very young, my mother planted in me the seed of compassion by the example she set. She raised me on a diet of love.

It was often my job to collect the eggs from our hens. I took my duty very seriously.

While my mother cooked, the aroma of korey—a delicious bread—wafting from our kitchen, I would play in the courtyard with scorpions for company.

Sometimes I would sit on the roof of our house. It was the perfect place to watch the mountains reach toward the sky. I'd imagine what the older boys were doing as they accompanied their fathers herding. I couldn't wait to be big enough to do that.

My other favorite perch was atop my mother's shoulders. From there I felt like one of the older boys. I was taller than my father! And getting around was so easy: When I wanted to go left, I would simply tug on my mother's left ear. When I wanted to go right, I would give her right ear a pull. And if she didn't understand my instructions, or chose to ignore them, I would kick, kick, KICK my legs!

Although my mother could not teach me to read or write, I learned so much from her. I was often a naughty boy, but she always treated me with kindness. Sometimes I think she may have been a little too patient with me—I was a bit spoiled!

But that was her nature. She was this way with everyone around her. One year when there was a famine in our region and many families did not have enough to eat, my mother gave whatever food we had stored to our neighbors and those in need.

In this way, she tended the seed of that most important lesson by demonstrating how to practice compassion. She showed me as a child that it was possible to treat all people with warmheartedness and to help ease their suffering.

Like a tall tree never forgets the seed it sprouted from, I've often returned to the seed of compassion my mother planted, and which I carried with me—as a small child at home, as a young monk in training, and today, as I spread the message of compassion around the world.

I loved growing up under the big open sky in Taktser. But I always knew that my life would take me beyond my small village.

When I was almost three, some monks came from the capital, Lhasa, looking for the child who was the reincarnation of the Dalai Lama, the spiritual leader of the Tibetan Buddhists. They had been searching all over the country for him, and the millions of people of Tibet had been waiting to hear that he had been found.

No one in my family could have expected that I was that child. Least of all me. But after passing a series of tests where I correctly identified the belongings of the previous Dalai Lama and held them with a great sense of familiarity, our visitors were satisfied that they had found the boy they were looking for.

And so, at age four, I made the journey to Lhasa in a caravan that snaked through the mountains. It took three months, and as news spread that the new Dalai Lama had been found, more and more people joined the procession.

I rode in a beautiful palanquin with my brother. We were rambunctious boys, and every time we roughhoused inside the cozy cabin, we would knock it off balance. We had to be separated for the rest of the journey!

In Lhasa, after I turned six, my formal education began and my days were filled with studies. In the few hours I had for personal time, I loved to puzzle over how things worked. I could spend hours taking apart toys, clocks, and watches and putting them back together again or exploring the mechanics of movie projectors and cars.

This occasionally got me in trouble.

As I trained to be a monk, I studied many subjects, like Buddhist philosophy and history, logic and reasoning, metaphysics, poetry, medicine, Tibetan, and Sanskrit.

One topic that I loved was compassion, because of the seed that had been planted by my mother. I believe that is what led me to free the people held in the prison next to Potala Palace, where I lived.

I have spent my entire life studying this topic and I know it is my duty to help make the world a more compassionate place.

The remarkable thing is, this ability is within every one of us, and it is strongest, I believe, within children like you.

Many Buddhist teachings compare those on the journey of life to sprouts, or the young shoots of a plant that must be tended until they grow strong and thrive. Parents often describe their children as sprouts too, especially when they see how quickly they grow!

But children are like sprouts not just physically, but in how they contain potential that can be nourished. The seed of compassion is within every child. It is there from birth and is a part of our nature. And it flourishes because of love.

If you think about it, when it comes to the five basic senses, we humans are not all that impressive.

The elephant has a long nose and can pick up faint scents from much greater distances than we can.

The hare can turn his tall ears forward and backward to pick up sounds that we would miss.

The eagle has eyes that can spot the tiniest prey from far up in the sky.

It's not the use of our senses that makes us special.

But only humans have the ability, with discipline and effort, to train the mind. It is what makes us different from all other animals.

It is our superpower.

And it is where the seed of compassion thrives.

Think about this: When you are playing in the schoolyard and a group welcomes you with a smile, do you want to play with them? Or do you want to play with someone who greets you with a scowl?

Of course you want to play with someone who welcomes you with a genuine smile, as you already have the ability to see genuine compassion in others.

From self-confidence grows compassion, and from compassion strength blooms.

But so often our world puts importance on material things and pushes us to be competitive with the people around us. The material world is based only in the five basic senses. Compassion is based in the mind, the part of us that is uniquely human. It is where you might grow strongest and how you can *create* something positive in the world. Because compassion is not a sign of weakness— it is a sign of strength.

When you approach someone with true warmheartedness, they can feel it. Doing so only brings more joy to you *and* them.

There are many simple ways to bring more happiness to the world.

But you already know that. What you must do now is protect and nurture this seed.

When someone disagrees with you, rather than think they are mistaken, you must ask, *Why might they feel this way?*

When someone is scowling or upset or hurt, you could busy yourself with your own concerns, or you could ask, *What might I do to help them?*

These questions may not come immediately. But just as you gradually learn to read, or swim, or play an instrument, you can build compassion day by day. It takes practice. And even when you slip and don't make the compassionate choice, tomorrow presents the opportunity for you to try again.

I have many responsibilities in my life, but helping to make the world a more compassionate place is the most important one. We cannot change the past. We can only learn from it. Otherwise, it is beyond our control. But the *future* we can change. And as children, you already have the tools needed to build a happier world, a better world, a compassionate world.

TIMELINE OF HIS HOLINESS THE 14TH DALAI LAMA'S LIFE

- **JULY 6, 1935** Born in Taktser, Amdo, Tibet.

- **JULY 1939** Departs Amdo for Lhasa, the capital of Tibet.

- **FEBRUARY 22, 1940** Enthronement ceremony officially recognizing him as the 14th Dalai Lama. Soon after, he begins his studies as a monk. He splits his time between Norbulingka, the summer residence of the Dalai Lama, and Potala Palace, the winter residence of the Dalai Lama and the seat of the Tibetan government.

- **NOVEMBER 17, 1950** At age 15, assumes the additional role as the political leader of the Tibetan people.

- **MARCH 17, 1959** Escapes to India following the brutal suppression of the Tibetan national uprising in Lhasa by Chinese troops.

- **DECEMBER 10, 1989** Receives the Nobel Peace Prize.

- **MAY 29, 2011** Formally relinquishes his role as the political leader of Tibet and transfers that authority to elected leaders.